THE STORY OF JOE BIDEN

A Biography Book for New Readers

Written by
Frank Berrios

Illustrated by
Alessandra Santelli

ROCKRIDGE PRESS

To my uncle Mike, and all the men and women in my family who proudly served our country.

For general information on our other products and services or to obtain technical support, please contact our Customer Care Department within the United States at (866) 744-2665, or outside the United States at (510) 253-0500.

Rockridge Press publishes its books in a variety of electronic and print formats. Some content that appears in print may not be available in electronic books, and vice versa.

Series Designer: Angela Navarra
Interior and Cover Designer: Lisa Schreiber
Art Producer: Hannah Dickerson
Editor: Eliza Kirby
Production Editor: Jenna Dutton
Production Manager: Giraud Lorber

ISBN: Print 978-1-64876-716-6 | eBook 978-1-64876-536-0
R0

Printed in China

CONTENTS

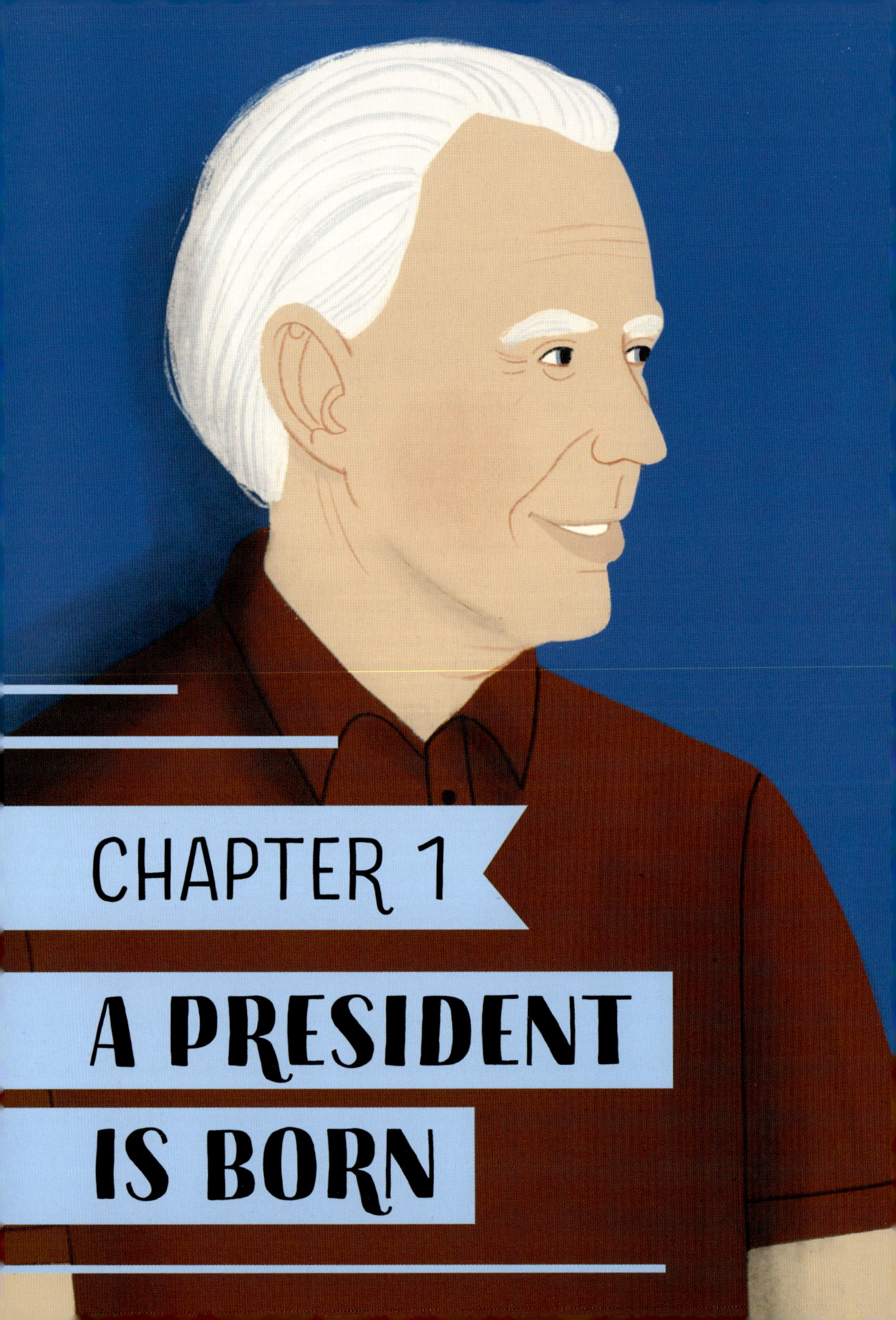

CHAPTER 1

A PRESIDENT IS BORN

Meet Joe Biden

Joe Biden is a **politician** who has worked to make America, and the entire world, a better place to live. Joe was first **elected** to represent the people of Delaware in 1972. He was only 30 years old, which made him one of the youngest **senators** in US history. He was reelected to the Senate six times and served more than 35 years before Barack Obama selected him to be vice president in 2008. Now, Joe has become the 46th president of the United States of America!

As a boy, Joe had a **stutter**, which made it difficult for him to speak. Some kids teased Joe when they heard him talk. Joe didn't like to be teased, so he stood up to those bullies. He learned that it was wrong to be mean to others just because they were different. Joe eventually gained the confidence to be a leader and to defend people who couldn't defend themselves—which he is still doing today.

Life hasn't always been easy for Joe. But every time he was knocked down, Joe got right back up. So, let's learn more about the incredible journey of Joe Biden, from a little boy with a stutter to the 46th president!

Joe's America

Joseph Robinette Biden Jr. was born in Scranton, Pennsylvania, on November 20, 1942. Scranton was a great place for a kid to grow up in the 1940s. As children, Joe and his friends would spend their days riding bikes, playing sports, or exploring the neighborhood. They would wander down to the local shops for candy and ice cream, or spend Saturdays at the movie theater.

Like most of the people in his neighborhood, Joe was **Catholic**. On Sundays, Joe and his family would start their day at church. Joe was inspired by the lessons he learned from the **Bible**. His parents, grandparents, uncles, and aunts also taught him lessons about life that would shape his future.

Although Joe lost an uncle in World War II, life was otherwise pretty good for him. But things weren't so great for all Americans.

> "The art of living is simply getting up after you've been knocked down."

During this time, many places in the United States were **segregated**. People of color weren't allowed to live wherever they wanted to live. Instead, lots of places had neighborhoods for white people only. Many stores and businesses were also segregated, so it was hard for nonwhite people to find good jobs. Some restaurants even refused to serve Black customers. As a warning, they placed

JUMP IN THE THINK TANK

How can you make your world a better place? Are you kind to others? Do you remember to reuse and recycle?

"WHITE CUSTOMERS ONLY" signs in their windows. Joe began to notice these terrible things. He wondered if they could ever change. He began to think of ways he could make this country a better place for everyone who called it home.

WHEN?

1941 — The United States enters World War II.

1942 — Joe is born in Scranton, Pennsylvania.

1945 — World War II ends.

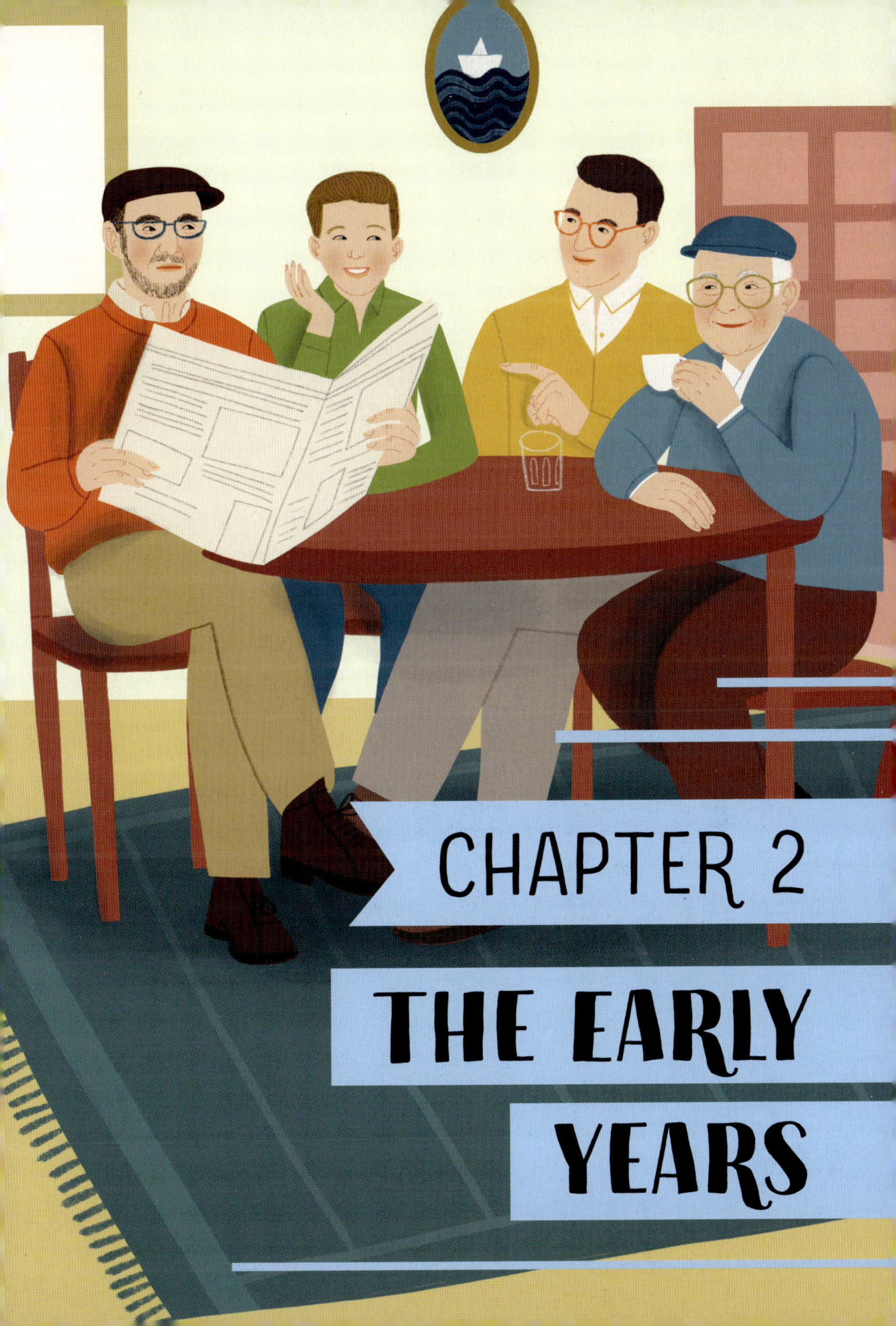

CHAPTER 2
THE EARLY YEARS

Growing Up the Biden Way

Joe, or Joey as he was known back then, had an ordinary childhood. He would often listen to his uncles and aunts talk about sports, **politics**, and world events as they sat around the kitchen table. Joe learned a lot from his family. His grandpop taught him to always keep his word.

The Biden Family

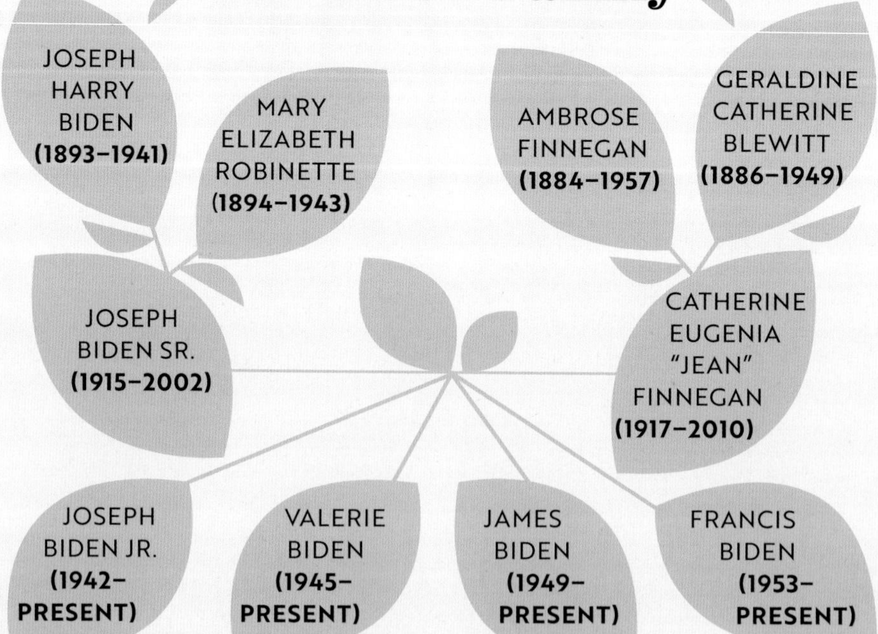

His mother made sure he treated everyone with respect. "You're not better than anybody else, but *nobody* is better than you," she told Joe. His father taught him to work hard and tell the truth.

As the oldest of four children, Joe also had to learn how to share with his younger brothers, Jim and Frank, and his sister, Valerie. Since they were only a few years apart in age, Joe and Val were like best friends. They rode bikes, played games, and went almost everywhere together.

Joe's father worked long hours, but he always made sure to be home for dinner with his wife and kids. He sold used cars and had a small job at a farmers' market. He even cleaned boilers and furnaces for a while. Joe's dad proudly did any job he could find to care for his family.

During this time, Joe was teased about his stutter. Kids nicknamed him "Dash" because his speech sounded like the dot-dot-dash-dash of **Morse code**. Joe would never forget how it felt to be treated badly because he didn't express himself like everyone else.

MYTH & FACT

MYTH: People who stutter aren't smart.

FACT: No one speaks perfectly all the time. Stuttering has nothing to do with how smart you are.

Making a Wish Come True

JUMP IN THE THINK TANK

What kind of school would you like to go to—a big school, a small school, or an online school?

Joe's family moved to Delaware when Joe was 10 years old. It was hard for Joe to leave his old buddies behind, but he quickly made new friends. More importantly, Joe began to dream about his future. It all started with Archmere Academy. To some people, Archmere was just another Catholic school. But to Joe, the building was a work of art. Although his family couldn't afford the **tuition**, Joe continued to dream about the school. When he learned there was a work-study program that would help him pay for school, Joe applied and was accepted. During the summer, Joe and several other students tended the gardens, painted fences, and cleaned more windows than they could count.

Joe's first few days at Archmere were great. But Joe was the second-smallest student at the school. Soon, the other kids also noticed his stutter. Joe practiced his speech each night. He read poems out loud while looking in the mirror. Soon, he stuttered less and less.

By his junior year, Joe had grown a whole foot taller. He was also a talented football player. His amazing ability to catch the ball earned him a new nickname: Hands. During his junior and senior years, Joe was elected class president!

Still, Joe never forgot what it felt like to be teased. As class president, he looked out for the students who didn't fit in. After four years, Joe was excited to go to college.

WHERE?

WHEN?

1953	1959	1960	1961
Joe and his family move to Delaware.	Joe is elected class president.	John F. Kennedy is elected president of the US.	Joe graduates from Archmere Academy.

CHAPTER 3
THE START OF SOMETHING BIG

★ Making Moves ★

Joe continued to play football at the University of Delaware, and he enjoyed meeting new people. He was excited to be elected president of his class again. For Joe, it was another small step toward public office like one of his heroes, John F. Kennedy, the 35th president of the United States.

Joe had followed Kennedy's career in politics. He listened closely to his **inauguration** speech in 1961. Kennedy's words echoed lessons that Joe had learned at home, school, and church. He truly began to believe it was his duty to make the world a better place.

> "If you put your mind to something, there's **nothing you can't do.**"

One summer, Joe got a job at a public pool in an all-Black neighborhood. As the only white lifeguard, he saw that **racism** was a huge problem. He began to agree with leaders like Dr. Martin Luther King Jr., who demanded **civil rights** and equal treatment for all people. Back in high school, when the owner of a local restaurant refused to serve his African American teammate, Joe and his friends stormed out. Joe's family and faith had taught him that all people are created equal.

Meanwhile, on a spring break vacation, Joe spotted a lovely woman sitting beside the pool. Her name was Neilia Hunter. Joe said hello, and the two decided to go on a date. That night, Joe felt like his feet never touched the ground! After the trip, Joe raced home to tell his family that he had found the woman he would marry.

After graduation, Joe applied to Syracuse University College of Law, just down the road from Neilia's childhood home. The two got married weeks after the end of Joe's first year of law school.

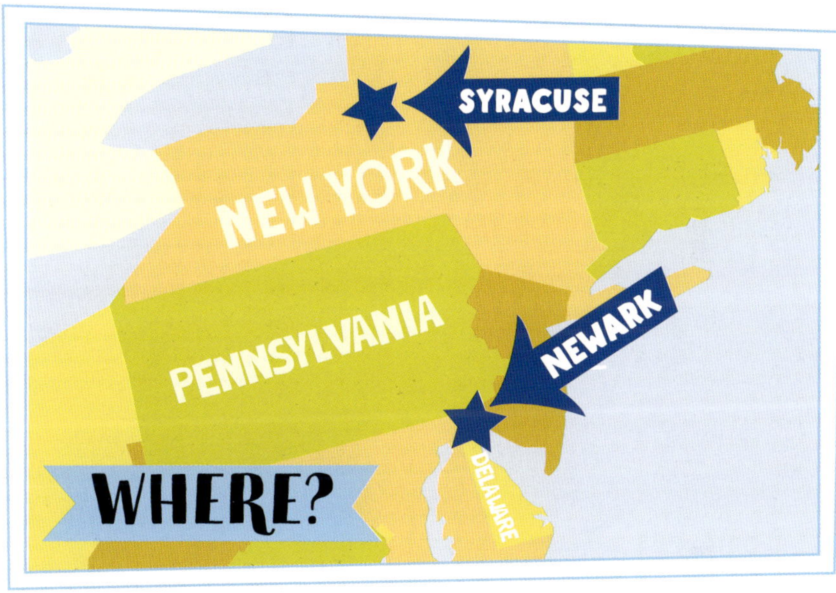

Joining the Democratic Party

In 1968, Joe began his career as a **lawyer**. With help from his father, Joe got a good-paying job with a law firm. Most of their cases involved big clients with lots of money, like railroad, oil, and construction companies. Joe didn't like the work very much. Instead of pushing to get more money for the big companies, Joe felt like he should be fighting to help hardworking Americans make enough money and keep their jobs. That's when he decided to become a public defender. A public defender is a lawyer who works for people who cannot afford to hire their

own lawyer. Most of Joe's clients were good people in need of a little help during tough times.

Meanwhile, some of Joe's **Republican** friends asked him to join their political party. A political party is a group of people who have the same ideas about what the government should do. But Joe declined. He was a **Democrat** like his hero John F. Kennedy. Kennedy had been the first Catholic president of the United States. That made Joe, and his Irish Catholic mom, very proud. More importantly, Kennedy supported the **civil rights movement**, which was led by another one of Joe's heroes, Dr. Martin Luther King Jr. After joining the Democratic party, Joe got more involved in politics.

JUMP IN THE THINK TANK

Who do you look up to? A parent, grandparent, teacher, or neighbor? A big brother, little sister, or best friend?

Joe and Neilia also became parents in 1969 with the birth of their first son, Joseph, who they nicknamed Beau. Joe's public life had barely begun, but already his dreams were starting to come true!

WHEN?

1965 — Joe graduates from the University of Delaware.

1966 — Joe starts law school and marries Neilia Hunter.

1968 — Joe becomes a lawyer.

1969 — Joe's first son, Beau, is born.

CHAPTER 4

SENATOR BIDEN

Let the Elections Begin!

A year after Beau was born, Neilia gave birth to another son, Hunter. And the next year, their daughter, Naomi, was born. Around that time, Joe was asked to run for a seat on the county council. People on the county council make decisions about where to build new homes, roads, and schools. Joe wasn't sure he had time to be a county councilman and didn't think he could win. Still, he entered the race. Joe promised to fight for what mattered to everyday Americans. No one expected a Democrat like Joe to win, because the voters in that area were mostly Republican. But to everyone's surprise, Joe won by more than 2,000 votes!

In 1972, Joe was asked to help find a strong Democratic **candidate** for the US Senate. The current Republican senator was extremely popular and hadn't lost an election in Delaware in more than 25 years. Joe thought about running himself. Many people thought Joe was too inexperienced to be a senator. Plus, US senators must be at least 30 years old, and Joe was only 29. If Joe won, he would be 30 by the time he was **sworn in**—so he decided to run! Joe's campaign was a family project. Everyone from Neilia to his siblings pitched in. His sister, Val, was his campaign manager. Joe's younger brothers, Jimmy and Frankie, helped pass out flyers. After a hard-fought campaign, Joe shocked everyone again by winning!

JUMP IN THE THINK TANK

Do you get nervous or scared about trying something new?

Sadly, a few weeks later, Joe's family was in a terrible car accident. Joe's wife and daughter passed away. His sons were also hurt in the crash, but thankfully, they survived. Joe was heartbroken, but he owed it to Neilia to carry on with his work. Soon, Joe was sworn in as a US senator.

The United States Senate

When Joe first arrived in Washington, DC, he was still very young. Most people didn't know he was actually a senator. Joe would often get stopped by security guards who asked to see his **identification**. "Senators only, young fella," they warned as he walked to the elevators. Joe was determined to do the best job he could, but after the accident, he wasn't sure he still wanted to be a senator. Thankfully, many other senators, both Democrats and Republicans, reached out to him to offer friendship and advice.

Before long, Joe settled into the work. Over his long career, he fought for and against many issues. He was against the Vietnam War, which he thought was a waste of time, money, and lives. He supported a woman's right to be paid the same amount as a man for doing the same job. He also battled to protect the environment.

MYTH	& FACT
Men and women are paid the same amount for the same work.	Even today, women are often paid less than men for the exact same job.

When Joe wasn't working, he was taking the train back and forth to Delaware to be with Beau and Hunter. Instead of moving the boys to Washington, he decided to keep them close to their grandparents and cousins in Delaware. Joe's sister, Val, moved into his house to help raise the boys.

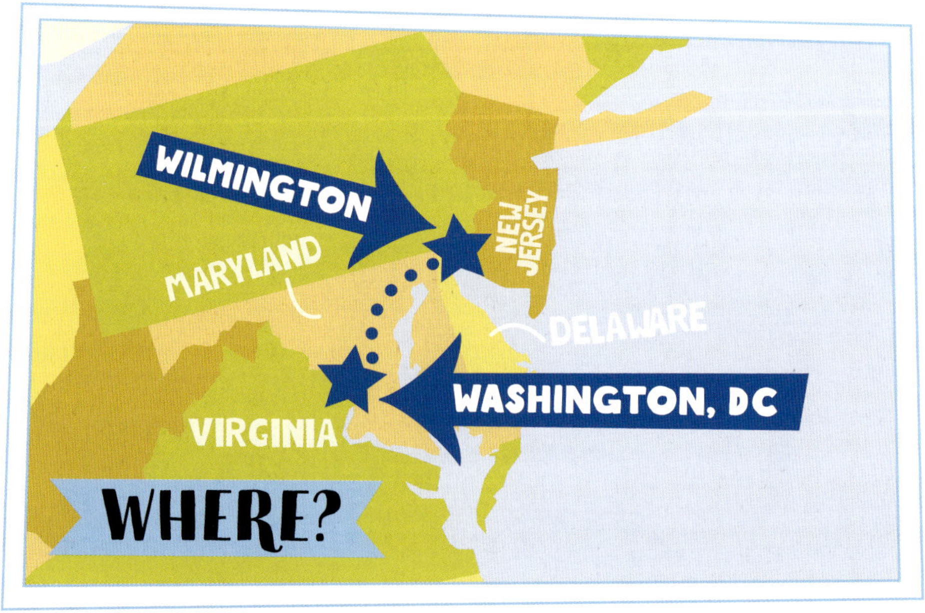
WILMINGTON
NEW JERSEY
MARYLAND
DELAWARE
WASHINGTON, DC
VIRGINIA
WHERE?

In 1975, Joe met a teacher named Jill Jacobs. No one could replace Neilia, but Joe realized that Jill made him feel happy again. The couple fell in love and were married in New York City. Not long after, they had a baby girl named Ashley.

WHEN?

1970	Joe becomes a county councilman.
1970	Joe's second son, Robert Hunter, is born.
1971	Joe's first daughter, Naomi, is born.
1972	Joe becomes a US senator.
1977	Joe marries Jill Jacobs.
1981	Joe and Jill's daughter, Ashley, is born.

CHAPTER 5
MEANT TO BE

Setting Sights on the White House

Joe proudly served in the Senate for more than 35 years. He tried to become president of the United States in 1988, but he didn't win the **nomination**. The presidential election process starts with smaller elections in each state, called primary elections. Primary elections are a way for each party to choose the person they think should represent them in the general election. Anyone can choose to run for president, but each party can only nominate one person to represent them.

In 2007, Joe decided to run for president again. He hit the campaign trail and discussed his ideas with voters. He wanted to make sure Americans were safe and healthy, so he shared ideas about how to reduce crime and increase funding for health care. He also wanted to bring American troops home from the war in Iraq. Many people respected Joe's ideas, including Senator Barack Obama.

MYTH & FACT

Myth: Once a senator is elected, they have that job for their whole life.

Fact: Senators have to win a new election every six years if they want to stay in the Senate. Joe won seven Senate elections!

Barack Obama was also running for president in 2008. Like Joe, he hoped to be the Democratic nominee. Joe and Barack had different styles, but they also had a lot in common. They were both lawyers before joining the Senate. They both became senators when they were young and had fresh ideas.

Joe had many years of experience as a senator. Barack had only two. But Barack knew younger voters wanted something different. Barack's message was one of change. It was hard for Joe to push back against Barack's message to new voters.

When Barack won the Democratic Party nomination, he needed a running mate with experience and connections in Washington. Joe was the perfect choice to be his vice president!

JUMP IN THE THINK TANK

Sometimes changes, like a new home or school, can be scary. But change can also be good! If you could, would you change anything in your life?

Campaigning for Vice President

Many people were excited when Barack became the very first African American nominee for president. The country had come a long way since the civil rights era. Even though it was a crime to discriminate against people based on the color of their skin, many people of color still

struggled to find good jobs and decent homes. There was work to be done. Joe hoped that Barack's nomination was a sign that things were finally starting to change in America. He was proud to be Barack's running mate.

Joe and Barack were a great team on the campaign trail. Joe enjoyed meeting new people, and he seemed to have endless energy. As they crisscrossed the nation, spreading a message of hope and change, Joe would often stay behind to shake hands or share ideas after his speeches.

The Obama/Biden campaign slogan, "Change We Can Believe In," inspired young and old voters alike. Their supporters were people of all races and religions. People flocked to hear their plans for a better future. In each new town and city, eager chants of "Yes We Can" grew louder and louder as Joe and Barack took the stage.

When the votes came in on election night, Joe was overjoyed. Barack Obama would become the 44th president of the United States—and Joe would join him as vice president!

> "Progress is **never easy**, but it is **always possible.**"

WHEN?

2007	2008	2008	2009
Joe starts his presidential campaign.	Barack Obama selects Joe to be vice president.	Barack and Joe win the general election.	Barack and Joe are sworn in.

CHAPTER 6

VICE PRESIDENT BIDEN

Giving His All

Working with President Barack Obama in the White House was inspiring and rewarding for Joe. They had learned a lot about each other and grown much closer on the campaign trail. Now it was time to roll up their sleeves and get to work!

The first thing to work on was the **economy**. In 2008, there was a big economic crisis and people all over the world lost their jobs and homes. A month after Barack and Joe were sworn into office, they quickly supported the Recovery Act, which helped businesses create new jobs across the country. Next up was the Affordable Care Act. Barack and Joe believed that every American should have health care. They created the Affordable Care Act to make it cheaper and easier to see a doctor if you got sick.

Barack valued Joe's advice and experience. Joe was often the last one in the office with

Barack before he made a difficult decision about the country. And in 2012, Barack and Joe were reelected for another four years!

Near the end of their time together in office, Barack said Joe was "the best vice president America's ever had." He gave Joe the Presidential Medal of Freedom, which is the highest civilian award a person can earn.

Sadly, in 2015, Joe's oldest son, Beau, died of cancer. Joe was heartbroken, but his faith and family helped him in this hard time.

The country had grown to know and love Joe during his eight years in the White House. Many expected him to run for president in 2016, but Joe decided not to run. Instead, he wanted to spend time with his family.

New Life, New Challenges

It was hard for Joe to relax after he left the White House in 2017. Even though he was no longer the vice president, he felt the need to stay active in the community. Joe started the Biden Foundation to help people get better education and better jobs, which would help them improve their lives.

MYTH & FACT

MYTH: People like to relax when they retire.

FACT: Some people, like Joe, become even busier in retirement!

JUMP —IN THE— THINK TANK

Joe wanted to share his knowledge about the world, so he decided to teach at a college. Do you have a favorite teacher or subject?

Joe also became a professor at the University of Pennsylvania. He created the Penn Biden Center to show that strong relationships with other countries make America, and the world, a safer place.

As a tribute to his son Beau, Joe started the Biden Cancer Initiative, which brought together the greatest minds to research a cure for cancer. But Joe wasn't all work—he and Jill

always made time for their kids and grandkids. They also continued to travel whenever they could. They especially enjoyed their Nantucket Thanksgiving trip every year.

Joe was never one to stay quiet, so he continued to speak up if he saw someone using their power to harm others. If he noticed someone doing something wrong, he made his opinion known.

After a long discussion with his family in 2019, Joe announced that once again, he would run for president. In Joe's eyes, the country had lost its way. As always, Joe had some ideas on how to make things better. The best way to do that was from the White House.

WHEN?

2012	Barack and Joe win a second term.
2015	Joe's oldest son, Beau, dies.
2017	Joe receives the Presidential Medal of Freedom.
2017	Barack and Joe leave the White House.
2017	Joe becomes a professor at the University of Pennsylvania.
2019	Joe begins his presidential campaign.

CHAPTER 7

BECOMING PRESIDENT

★ Back in the Race ★

Joe started to campaign for president in 2020. But early that year, the world began to deal with a new **disease** called COVID-19. It was very **contagious**. Anyone could easily get sick if someone with the disease was near them. Many countries asked people to stay inside or wear masks when they left the house. This was the best way to stop spreading COVID-19.

To stay healthy, most people had to stay home, and kids couldn't go to school. "CLOSED" signs popped up at business after business. Many workers lost their jobs. Sadly, a lot of people died from COVID-19. It was a hard time, but Joe had seen Americans step up in the past. As president, he knew he could get the country back on track. He wanted to remind America how much they could do when they pulled together.

> America is made of ordinary people capable of **extraordinary things.**

Joe was nominated as the Democratic candidate for president in June 2020. He would be running against President Donald Trump, who was elected in 2016. Joe picked Senator Kamala Harris as his running mate. Joe and Kamala agreed on a lot of important issues. Kamala was also ready to make history. If elected, she would be the first woman, and the first person of color, to be vice president!

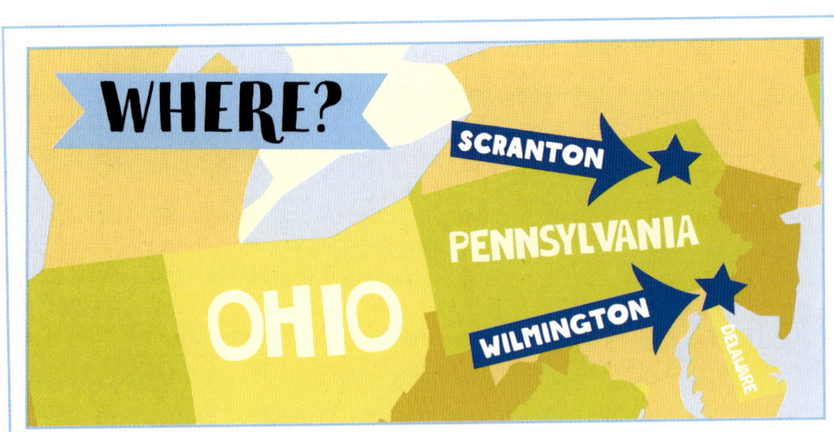

Because of COVID-19, Joe and Kamala had to campaign in a new way. Instead of flying around the country, as Joe had done in the past, they shared their ideas on TV and in online meetings with voters. It was different for Joe, but he hoped it would work.

JUMP IN THE THINK TANK

Americans always figure out a way to overcome obstacles. What gives you the strength to achieve your goals?

President Joe Biden

Some states allow people to vote before election day. Voters across the country started showing up early to vote for president. Many people had to wait in long lines. Others sent in their votes by mail. The country was still dealing with COVID-19, but Americans were determined to cast their votes.

Joe voted early in Delaware. On the morning of the election, he visited his church and the grave of his son Beau. Then he visited

his childhood home in Scranton, Pennsylvania. Inside, the owners asked him to sign a wall in their living room. "From this house to the White House with the grace of God," Joe wrote.

In 2020, Election Night was different from most elections. Usually, a winner is announced that night or early the next day, after all the votes are counted. But because so many people voted by mail, election officials knew they wouldn't be able to count all the votes in one night. They couldn't rush. They didn't want to make any mistakes.

Joe had run for office many times before, but this was the biggest election of his life. Like most Americans, he was excited and wanted to learn the results. Joe was patient, but also eager to tackle the problems facing the country. Finally, after four long days of counting, Joe was declared the winner! He would become the 46th president of the United States.

Joe was sworn in at the inauguration ceremony on January 20, 2021. Millions of people watched the inauguration on TV and online. Joe's many years in the Senate and his work as the vice president had prepared him for this moment—and he was ready for the challenge!

WHEN?

First case of COVID-19 is diagnosed in the US.	Joe wins the general election.	Joe and Kamala are sworn in.
2020	**2020**	**2021**

CHAPTER 8

SO . . . WHO IS JOE BIDEN?

Challenge Accepted!

Now that you have learned all about Joe Biden, let's test your new knowledge in a little who, what, when, where, why, and how quiz. Feel free to look back in the text to find the answers if you need to, but try to remember first!

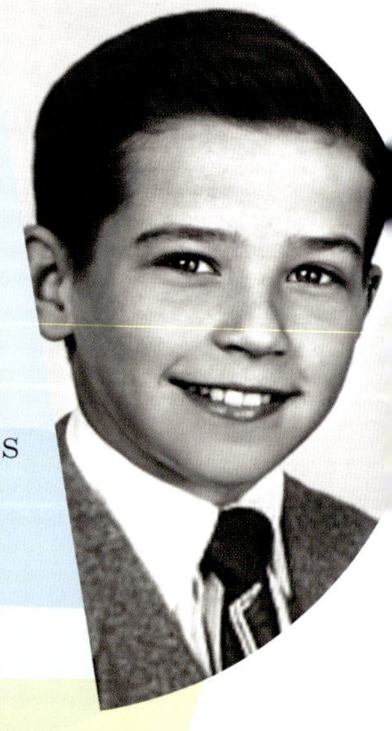

1 Who is Joe Biden?

→ A A former United States senator

→ B A former United States vice president

→ C The president of the United States

→ D All of the above

2 Where was Joe born?

→ A New York City

→ B Scranton, Pennsylvania

→ C Washington, DC

→ D Los Angeles, California

3 **How many brothers and sisters does Joe have?**

→ A 3

→ B 2

→ C 1

→ D 0

4 **What kind of work did Joe's father do?**

→ A He sold cars.

→ B He worked at a farmers' market.

→ C He cleaned boilers and furnaces.

→ D All of the above

5 **Where did Joe's family move when he was 10?**

→ A New Jersey

→ B New Hampshire

→ C South Carolina

→ D Delaware

6 **What was the name of the high school Joe attended?**

→ A McKinley High School
→ B Archmere Academy
→ C Cardozo High School
→ D Bel-Air Academy

7 **How old was Joe when voters elected him to the US Senate for the first time?**

→ A 29
→ B 33
→ C 37
→ D 44

8 **Who picked Joe to be his vice-presidential running mate in 2008?**

→ A John F. Kennedy Jr.
→ B Martin Luther King Jr.
→ C Barack Obama
→ D Mike Pence

9 **When was Joe elected president of the United States?**

→ A 1972

→ B 2008

→ C 2012

→ D 2020

10 **Who did Joe choose to be his vice-presidential running mate in 2020?**

→ A Barack Obama

→ B Kamala Harris

→ C Jill Jacobs

→ D Donald Trump

Answers: 1. D; 2. B; 3. A; 4. D; 5. D; 6. B; 7. A; 8. C; 9. D; 10. B

Our World

Joe has dedicated his entire life to making our world a safer, cleaner, and better place to live. In his more than 40 years of public service, Joe has fought to improve the lives of countless people around the globe.

→ Joe was one of the first senators to support a climate change bill to protect our planet. In 1987, he introduced the Global Climate Protection Act. This made a plan for the country to fight climate change.

→ Joe believes that everyone is created equal, so he stands against racism and **sexism**. He supports giving opportunities to every kind of person and fights for a woman's right to equal pay for equal work.

→ Joe brings countries around the world together to focus on common goals. He has traveled to war zones and seen the terrible things war brings. Joe pushes for peaceful solutions to all disagreements.

JUMP IN THE THINK TANK FOR MORE!

Joe liked to dream big. Even though his parents couldn't afford it, he found a way to get into the school of his dreams. When everyone thought he was too young and inexperienced to become a senator, he proved them wrong and won a tight race.

→ Joe always wanted to make the world a better place. Is there something about the world that you'd like to fix? What steps can you take to make it happen?

→ Joe's family has always been important to him. They've helped him with every election. How does your family support you and help you achieve your goals?

→ Working with people is a big part of Joe's job as president, and he believes in teamwork. Do you work well with others and enjoy being part of a team?

Glossary

Bible: A book of religious stories and prayers

candidate: A person who wants to be elected to a role in government

Catholic: A type of Christian faith

civil rights: Basic rights that every person has under the laws of the government to be treated fairly and equally

civil rights movement: A time of struggle during the 1950s and 1960s when Black people in the United States fought to end racial discrimination and have equal rights

contagious: When a sickness is spread between people

Democrat: A member of the Democratic political party

disease: A sickness

economy: A country's source of wealth and resources

elect: To pick someone by voting; the process is called an **election**, and the winner is **elected**

identification: A document or card that proves a person's name and date of birth

inauguration: The ceremony to mark the beginning of something, such as the beginning of a presidency

lawyer: A person who has studied the law and can represent other people or groups of people in court

Morse code: A code where letters are replaced by short and long lines or bursts of light or sound

nomination: The act of choosing a person for a job or award

politician: Someone whose job involves making decisions to run a government

politics: Activities related to the government of a city, state, country, or nation

racism: Discrimination against someone of a different race

Republican: A member of the Republican political party

segregated: Separated, and treated unfairly, usually based on skin color

senator: A person who is elected to represent their state in the Senate

sexism: Discrimination based on the belief that men are superior to women

stutter: When a person has difficulty speaking

sworn in: Officially took office by making a promise of honesty

tuition: The cost of a person's education

Bibliography

Biden, Jill. *Joey: The Story of Joe Biden*. New York: Flatiron Books, 2017.

Biden, Joseph R. *Promises to Keep: On Life and Politics*. New York: Random House, 2007.

———. *Promise Me, Dad: A Year of Hope, Hardship, and Purpose*. New York: Flatiron Books, 2017.

Harris, Kamala D. "About." Accessed December 28, 2020. Harris.Senate.gov/about.

Mejdrich, Kellie. "Biden Signs Wall of Childhood Home: 'From This House to the White House.'" *Politico*. November 3, 2020. Politico.com/news/2020/11/03/joe-biden-signs-wall-of-childhood-home-433933.

National Stuttering Association. "Stuttering Explained." Accessed December 28, 2020. WeStutter.org/what-is-stuttering.

The Obama White House. "President Obama Awards the Presidential Medal of Freedom to Vice President Biden." Video, 38:09. January 12, 2017. YouTube.com/watch?v=Qrz6Ge64hsc.

Osnos, Evan. *Joe Biden: The Life, the Run and What Matters Now*. New York: Scribner, 2020.

About the Author

FRANK BERRIOS is a writer born in New York City. He has written many books for children, including the following Little Golden Books: *Black Panther*, *Falcon*, and *Miles Morales: Spider-Man*, as well as *A Little Golden Book about Jackie Robinson*, *Football with Dad*, and *Soccer with Mom*. Learn more about his work at FrankBerriosBooks.com.

About the Illustrator

ALESSANDRA SANTELLI was born in a small city near Milan in 1990. She still lives there with her family and her huge cat, Michi. She grew up painting with tempera on the stones and making small illustrated books to sell to all her relatives. At that point it was fairly clear that she liked drawing, so she attended the Brera Fine Arts Academy in high school and the International Comics School. She currently collaborates with several Italian and foreign publishers and works in a studio that she opened with a colleague called Foglie al Vento. There, she likes to eat a lot of sweets while listening to David Bowie.